**Fitne**
**Pres**

# The 30-Day Mindset Shift Devotional

## Preparing for Purpose
## Volume I

By:

# Danielle Nicole Ramsey

# The 30-Day Mindset Shift Devotional

Preparing for Purpose

Volume I

# FitnessDani

## CHANGING LIVES INSIDE & OUT

A brand that
empowers & inspires
you to be the
best version of yourself.

www.FitnessDani.com

This book is dedicated to my mother, Gloria. She was the first person to believe in me and to make me feel as if I can do and accomplish anything in this world. She instilled in me great work ethic, self-worth, and the love of Christ.

Mom, I just simply want to thank you for being the best mother you could be to me. I'm anchored in my strength because of how you raised me. You will forever be my shero.

# Introduction

Before we go any further, let's start by congratulating yourself! Right here! Right now! Why you may ask?! Because, by holding this devotional in your hands, you have ALREADY made the decision that can take someone a lifetime to make! You've made the decision to change your way of thinking and work towards changing your mindset! That takes courage, vulnerability, and accountability!

## BRAVO!

As a matter of fact, you've already made two huge decisions already. One, the decision to want to change your mindset and Two, taking action by purchasing this devotional to help you along the way! So, let's see this thing through!

## Introduction Continued...

Over the next 30 days, get ready to embark on a journey that will have you so much closer to not just a mindset shift, but COMPLETELY evolving your way of thinking to help you become the best version of yourself! And, authentically!

Throughout this journey, do not expect perfect days, but days where you know you are giving 100% of yourself, and always remember to extend yourself grace each day.

Are you excited yet?! I sure hope you are because I am BEYOND excited for you!

The next page is your new beginning! I'm ready when you are!

# Day One

"...and that you be renewed in
the spirit of the mind..."
Ephesians 4:23

## Devotional I

Ahhh! There is nothing like a fresh start! A time to give yourself another chance, to give yourself a clean slate, a "Day One" if you will! Your momentum is high, your adrenaline is pumping, you get prepared, and then it's time to take off! You say to yourself, "This time, I'm going to see this thing through! This time is different! This time, I'm READY!" And guess what? You may very well be all of those things and yes, it is VERY exciting. But a renewed mind doesn't just come with motivation and excitement, it comes by mentally preparing yourself that there are absolutely no half-stepping days, that you will do what's necessary even when the motivation declines, and making it a nonnegotiable to show-up for yourself each day! Will it be challenging, YES, without a doubt, but when you surrender your mind to God, He will make these days more enjoyable than you can imagine!

## Activity I

For 15 minutes, I want you to find a tune that relaxes your mind, body and soul. Sit with candles lit, blocking out all distractions, and meditate and pray, spending quiet, intimate, alone time with God. You can repeat this activity as many times as you would like through this journey.

# End of Day Thoughts

# Day Two

"Our greatest battles are that
with our own minds?"
Jameson Fran

## Devotional II

You ever heard of the scripture that says, "As a man thinketh in his heart, so is he…"? It's so true! Whatever you think and feel about yourself will undoubtedly become the reality of how you treat yourself! Some days we feel unstoppable, like we can conquer the world and while the other days we can feel as if we don't have what it takes to change our circumstances. I've been there MANY times before and it's no fun. If we think about it, we tell ourselves no before even attempting to make a move towards what we want so badly because in our minds, we have already told ourselves that we can't, its impossible and/or we don't feel as if we are good enough. That ends today! You are

EVERYTHING God says you are! Walk in that truth and have FAITH that your desires will come to pass. It sounds easier said than done, but it CAN BE DONE. At this very moment, tell yourself that today is the day! The day where you stop self-sabotaging your dreams and give yourself a chance at what God has placed on your heart to fulfill. Own it. Work hard and always, always believe in yourself. You can do ANYTHING you put your mind to, if you're willing to work hard for it with no excuses and stay consistent with. God believes in you and I believe in you. You have everything it takes to achieve it all.

## Activity II

1. Write down 3 goals that you want to achieve this year.

2. Pray over them and ask God for guidance.

3. Research 3 things for each goal that will bring you closer to helping you achieve them.

# End of Day Thoughts

# Day Three

"If you think you can do a thing or think you can't do a thing, you're right."
Henry Ford

## Devotional III

I remember taking a job in Property Management, thinking that it was similar to Hotel Management. Because I had experience in hospitality, I applied to be a Property Manager of a multi-family community with more than 200 units. "This will be easy," I thought to myself. "I got this!" Very quickly after taking the position, I would soon find out that it was NOT easy and I did not have it! Property management was extremely challenging and I felt I was over my head. When the demands of my new role started to get to me, I felt as if I could not do the job and wanted to quit. I felt as if it was just too challenging for me and that I would never understand what I was doing. I went to work everyday with that mindset, making it unbearable to want to be there. I had gotten so far in my head that I started to make myself feel as if I did not belong there. Until one day. My regional manager came to visit me when I sent a request in to speak with him. That day, I planned on quitting and moving on, but our meeting changed my mind. He had told me that I was phenomenal at my job, a fast learner, I was coachable and I had the drive that was needed to be successful. He also told me to take it easy on myself and to not expect to be an expert being so new to the field, and that I was on the right track. That talk made me feel so good inside because I thought I sucked. Turns out, I didn't. From that day on, I started to change my thoughts about my job load and embrace being a student again. I said to myself, "If I'm going to be a student, I'm going to be an A+ student and learn all that I could. I did just that! My job became second nature after a while, the reports weren't intimidating anymore and I knew how to handle challenges with my tenants. One day at a time and a changed mindset is why I began to thrive. Same goes for you! What ever you think you can't do, tell yourself that you CAN! Don't allow fear, intimidation, or comfortability to keep you from growing in success! An "I CAN" attitude will take you very far!

## Activity III

What is something that you've told yourself over and over again that you can't do? Today, DO IT! Don't give yourself any excuses and just GO FOR IT! You might just surprise yourself.

# End of Day Thoughts

# Day Four

"Embrace the uncomfortable
to become unstoppable."
Sarah Jakes Roberts

## Devotional IV

No doubt. Being uncomfortable is well... uncomfortable. No one wakes up and decides that they want to feel this way. But, have you ever seen someone that's in their comfort zone being stretched to become extraordinary? Probably not. That's because becoming a FORCE in this world takes making HUGE leaps and bounds while having a ton of FAITH in God and TRUST in yourself! A lot of times we have one or the other, Faith in God and absolutely no trust in ourselves or the other way around. Being comfortable is such a vague statement. You want to be comfortable in your relationships, on your job, and in life in general, but not to the point where you aren't challenging yourself to be your very best. Comfortable is easy. It doesn't require much work, not much to think about, and the day to day is just that. But once you decide you want to challenge yourself, answer to the calling God has on your life and to live outside your comfort zone, you will indeed be tested in faith, tenacity, consistency and so many other things. Let me tell you, it's ALL worth it! Nothing worth having comes easy. It takes discipline, hard work and belief in yourself that you can achieve whatever you want. Once you have your first taste in succeeding while being uncomfortable, you'll keep challenging yourself, setting bigger goals, seeing that you have become a force in this world doing all the things you never thought you could! Keep going!

# Activity IV

1. Add 10 minutes to your cardio routine.

2. Unplug from all social media today and focus on your goals.

# End of Day Thoughts

# Day Five

"It is in the small decisions you and I
make everyday that creates our destiny."
Tony Robbins

## Devotional V

We all have life goals. Achieving those goals takes planning, follow through and daily action. You have to decide that the life goals that you have for yourself are of the utmost importance to you, and when you do, you will have to understand that your every day decisions, big and small, will affect how you shape your life.

Today, reading this devotional, you know in your heart if you've given yourself a real chance to create the life you want. Like a REAL chance. You would've created a vision board, followed through on goals you made on it and took action towards those goals every single day. Now, if you have…congratulations! That's major and should be celebrated! But, if you have not, decide TODAY, right now, that you will. Start small. Start with daily goals that turn into weekly goals that eventually will turn into monthly goals. Rome wasn't built in a day; it takes time to build a masterpiece. Be patient with yourself, you will make mistakes, but continue to push forward!

Each goal you achieve or complete, remember to celebrate yourself along the way! Every victory deserves a celebration.

## Activity V

1. Choose ONE goal that you want to focus on.

2. Create a vision board over this goal for the next 3 months.

# End of Day Thoughts

# Day Six

"I wake up every morning believing today
is going to be better than yesterday."
Will Smith

## Devotional VI

Every day that we wake up, we decide how we want our day to go. WE DECIDE; and the trajectory of that day starts with our thoughts. Be intentional with what you think about because your thoughts will soon be displayed in your life. Deciding to wake up bringing your best self is an intentional thought. You decide you're going to greet everyone you see with a smile; you're going to complete every project you start, and you're going to speak affirmations over your life every day, and hold yourself accountable when you justify an excuse you've made for yourself. Waking up with such a positive declaration will without a doubt set the tone for an amazing day to follow. After all, there is no point in dwelling over yesterday, it's already gone. But today, today will be better than the day before, because you decide it will be. You have more power than you think! Walk in that power and OWN the day! Start by thanking God for granting you another one.

# Activity VI

1.  Listen to a song that brings you happiness and joy.

2.  Buy a co-worker lunch.

3.  Find 3 old outfits in your closet you will never wear again and donate them.

# End of Day Thoughts

# Day Seven

"It does not matter how slowly you
go so long as you do not stop."
Confucious

## Devotional VII

If you're anything like me, you have started and stopped several things in your life before. A fitness journey, writing in a journal, projects that once motivated you about your future, etc. You name it, I've probably dabbled a few days in that as well. (insert laughing emoji) I can laugh about it now, and I shake my head at the thought of me completely STOPPING something that was very beneficial in my life. I've started and stopped so many fitness journeys I can't even begin to count how many. A fitness journey isn't a destination, but a marathon. There is no "end" …but only a continuation to becoming your best physical self. Exercise is something that we all take for granted. We should be excited that our body is at a functional state and that it allows us to do the things that makes us stronger while living a healthier life. Instead, we tend to act off motivation, get excited when we start to see results, and then eventually the motivation we once had starts to subside, we workout once or twice a week and then eventually not at all. The results we once saw are now fading and we are back at square one. How many times have you done this? If you answered honestly, you should probably be sick of yourself, just like I was. Enough is enough. Right?! You get to a place where this cycle HAS to end. And when it does, you no longer act off motivation, but are disciplined in to doing the things that are necessary to keep you going, whether you want to or not. Now, we all have our days where we may need a couple of days off, that's ok, that's part of the process. But, this time, we are going to keep going. One day at a time, rep at a time, breath at a time. We may take a break for a moment, but this time, we will NOT stop.

## Activity VII

During your workout today, when you feel yourself wanting to stop or if you are at the end of your workout, add 10 extra minutes to your cardio routine or add one extra set if you are strength training. You can do it! Anything you set your mind to, you can tackle! Own that workout and those bonus minutes and/or sets! You got this!

# End of Day Thoughts

# Day Eight

"Always do what you are
afraid of doing."
Ralph Waldo Emerson

## Devotional VIII

Nothing will keep us in the same place we so desperately want out of like fear. Fear will have and KEEP you stagnant forever, until YOU decide to make a move. When something is new to us or out of our comfort zones, usually, we will not go towards it and usually for two reasons. 1) Fear of the unknown. 2) Looking as if we don't know what we are doing. Well, this is something we have to get over because inevitably, if we are starting something new, we will never know what's on the other side until we place ourselves there and we ARE going to look as if we don't know what we are doing because, well, quite frankly, we don't! But guess what? That's OK! We aren't supposed to be experts starting ANYTHING new or foreign to us. We are students and are ready to learn! EVERYONE starts off as a student. No matter how old they are, how smart they may seem or the experience they may have. Instead of holding yourself back, learn to embrace the unknown and enjoy learning something new. A whole new world awaits once you stop allowing fear to control your life. Nine times out of ten, once you tap into that thing that you were once afraid of doing, you will find that it will be the best decision for your life and you will dive deeper wanting more. You will surprise yourself that you finally took the leap, but after that, it's game on! So today, whatever it is that you may be afraid of doing, DO IT! Even if you fail at this thing or find that it's not for you, you'll be happy knowing that you at least tried instead of saying you didn't at all. Perspective. Do it for YOU!

## Activity VIII

Name one thing that you have always wanted to do. Ask yourself why you're afraid to do it. Write it down. Pray over it. Take a step towards this thing and see how it makes you feel.

# End of Day Thoughts

# Day Nine

"Therefore, prepare your minds for
action, keep sober in spirit, fix your hope
completely on the grace to be brought to
you at the revelation of Jesus Christ."
1 Peter 1:13

## Devotional IX

Before I make any decision in my life these days, I
consult with my main man, Jesus. It is so important
to me that I continue to stay in alignment with my
purpose and to not make a detour to something that
may spark my interest, but will take me completely
off task. Sometimes, our minds can trick us into
thinking that the new thing that comes along aligns
with where we are going because it seems to have
all the bells and whistles that's needed, but just
like the old saying goes, "everything that glitters
isn't gold". Everything that SEEMS right, isn't. It's
important that we prepare for many detours while

on our destiny journey, and to remain steadfast in knowing that the difference between what seems and what is, is that what seems brings confusion and what IS brings clarity! "God is not the author of confusion, but of peace...". You will know the difference. You will feel it in your spirit. Don't ignore it, but pay attention. Often times when this happens, you're about to turn the corner on your journey and you're that much closer to being in your purpose. Stay the course. It's beyond worth it.

## Activity IX

Let's reflect: Remember when you detoured in your life when you were supposed to keep straight, but tried it your way? What are two things you have done and what did you learn from them?

# End of Day Thoughts

# Day Ten

"Do not call to mind the former things,
or ponder things of the past."
Isaiah 43:18

## Devotional X

Yesterday is gone and it will never be seen again. Our past is a part of our journey; it helps shape us into the people we are destined to be. But what we cannot do is live there. We already did. All the days of our past have been lived out in its entirety, and now, we live for the present day while following God's guidance to help us prepare for our future.

When thinking of the past, we often think of the mistakes we have made, the failures that can sometimes linger into our present day, or things we wish we could go back and rewrite…do over. When we do this, we are putting our growth at a standstill or may be still searching for a lesson that should have been learned. What ever it is, moving forward, when thinking of the past, think of how far you've come and rejoice in where God has you NOW. Now, is a blessing! Now, is here! Now, is your focus! We can't change the past, so there is no use in pondering over it. What we can do now is shape our future. We all have done things we aren't proud of, after all, we are only human, but forgive yourself, ask for God's forgiveness and move on. Don't say to yourself that it's easier said than done, because it's not. You can do anything with God by your side. When your past tries to creep in and remind you of the things you've already been forgiven for, remember this. I can do all things through Christ which strengthens me.

## Activity X

Write three things from your past that tries to stipple your future. Ask for forgiveness, and then forgive yourself. Now, write three things that you can implement in your life to turn you away from that.

# End of Day Thoughts

# Day Eleven

*"Believe you can...and you are halfway there!"*
Theodore Roosevelt

## Devotional XI

"Believe in yourself!" We've heard someone say this to us at LEAST 10x in our lifetime, I'm sure! But why? Why do you think people tell us to believe in ourselves? Is it because someone told them to do so and it made them feel good? Is it because you felt how good it felt and passed on the good feeling? Or maybe, just maybe, that when you believe in yourself, like TRULY believe, that you know that ALL things are possible?! I hope the last one was the reason you tell someone these 3 magical words, but if it isn't and you're still stuck between one and two, it's ok...we have all been there! Believing in yourself takes igniting your inner power and activating that with your outer being, collaborating the two and putting belief into practice...habit...a way of life if you will. And, when you believe that you can manifest all that God places in your heart, you are indeed, halfway there! Why is that?

Because when you believe in yourself, you believe in your ability to see past all failures, all hinderances and everything that tries to come along way that tells you that you can't and you still know that you can! Believing in yourself takes preparation, planning and steps towards a life that says you can have all that you are willing to work hard for! When these steps are taken, you are ultimately saying that your belief is activated and you're taking yourself to a place that you're wanting to see manifested. Keep going. Keep moving. And never stop believing.

## Activity XI

Speak these 3 affirmations over your life today. Say them everyday until you believe them and as many times as you want.

1. I believe in the abilities God has given me.

2. I believe in God's divine purpose for my life.

3. I believe in me and that I have more than enough to see these things through.

# End of Day Thoughts

# Day Twelve

"Imagination is more important
than knowledge. Knowledge is limited.
Imagination encircles the world."
"Imagination is everything. It is the
preview of life's coming attractions."
Albert Einstein

### Devotional XII

When I was a little girl, I used to imagine myself on a huge stage, in front of a huge crowd, making people smile and feel better about themselves. As a grown woman, I still have this same image in my head, except now, I can make out why the crowd is smiling back at me. For a far as I can remember, I knew that I wanted make a difference in this world. I knew that I wanted to touch the hearts of people and for everyone to feel as if they are someone in this world. I have always had a heart for people and wanting everyone to be happy. The older I got, the more I started to realize that happiness is an inside job. Someone can have a smile on their face but be unhappy on the inside. My vision slowly started to shift. I just didn't want smiling faces anymore, I wanted smiling hearts, too! My imagination now took me to a place of where I was talking to these people one by one and in front of a crowd. My vision that I had as a little girl was me on stage as a Motivational Speaker, and I was able to make that out when I was 33 years old and once, I did, I started to do my homework because I wanted this vision that I've had for most of my life to be a reality. I wanted to get on stage, touch the lives of others and make their hearts smile. I not only just want that to happen, I need that to happen. And it will. I know it will. But who knows, this book may be my stage and the audience could very well be the readers of this book, and if so, I say thank you Lord! And dwell in that alone! If He says this, is it, then it is so! Whether I'm on stage giving a motivational speech or the author of a devotional book...either way, I will think of the little girl with the vivid imagination, that saw out into the audience of people with smiles on their faces and know that at the end of this thing, that they too, will have smiles in their hearts as well.

## Activity XII

What was something that you have imagined as a child, or even as an adult? Use any space that you have in your house and act out that image. Make it come to life and enjoy every minute of it.

# End of Day Thoughts

# Day Thirteen

"It doesn't matter who you used
to be. All that matters is who
you're willing to become."
Sarah Jakes Roberts

## Devotional XIII

And one day, you just wake up...different. Not wanting the same old results. Not wanting to hold yourself back any longer. Not wanting to rest in the excuses you've justified for as long as you could remember. Oh no. You wanted to become a version of yourself that you had to challenge yourself to become. A challenge that would not come easy, but one that came with change, different results, a different mindset, honesty and absolutely no excuses. One where you were no longer in control, but you've surrendered yourself to your calling no matter how difficult the road may seem, you were willing to walk this road with God in front leading the way. When you're willing to become THIS version of yourself, you are now ready to live!

Getting to this version of yourself will be no cake walk. Everything that you thought will be challenged and you must let go. Left becomes right, south becomes north and your yes becomes no! But, it's all for a reason and bigger than any reason we could ever give ourselves. Deciding to turn away from what you know to what you don't, but are willing to learn will be one of the best decisions you'll ever make. Becoming what you no longer want to represent takes consistency, commitment, and determination to want the will to change. Everything you need to bring you to this place; you already have in you. Trust yourself, do the work and show up every day.

## Activity XIII

Name two things that you know you need to change about yourself in order to grow?

Take those two things, and write how you can eliminate them from your life.

# End of Day Thoughts

# Day Fourteen

"Do nothing from selfishness or empty conceit, but with humility of mind regard one another as more important than yourselves."
Philippians 2:3

### Devotional XIV

Giving. It's an art that I've come to absolutely love! Whether is paying for a stranger's food, buying a gift for a loved one, or simply just cleaning out my closet of things I no longer wear and gifting them to someone less fortunate. There is no better feeling you'll have than when you know you are blessing someone. God blesses us to BE a blessing, not to just keep things for ourselves. If I'm honest, I was not always this way. When it came to the things above, that came easy for me, but when it came to tithing, I was not a faithful tither. I would give here and there, and not even the 10% God asked of me, but something just to say I gave. This is crazy to think about now, but I justified me not giving with I didn't have enough money, or my church was pretty well off, they didn't need it or just not wanting to. I always felt convicted during offering time, but would try to ignore the feeling and think of something else. I wasn't intentionally trying to be selfish, I just wanted to hold on to the little bit of money that I did have. And it is with that mindset, while the little that I had, was the little that I was going to continue to have. God purposely allowed me to hear plenty of sermons on giving, and I would feel the urge to give, but then think about a bill or my expenses for the upcoming week and would give a little. "It's better than nothing" I used to say. And sure, something is better than nothing, but when you give from that place, you might as well not give at all. This continued on for a while until one day, I heard a sermon that completely changed it all for me. I had begun my surrendering journey with God and this was one of the first wrongs I wanted to make right. I remember how hard it was for me to give 10%. It seemed like so much at the time, but now, I only cared about doing the right thing and being obedient to His word. Before I knew it, tithing had gotten much easier and in fact, I looked forward to tithing. I felt good inside knowing that God was pleased with my obedience and that was all the validation I needed to keep going. This is how God wants us to be with one another as well. To not keep everything to ourselves, but to share our wealth, knowledge, life skills, etc. Together, we are better. The next time you have a chance to give, do it. And from the heart. You just never know what your good deed can do to bless someone else.

## Activity XIV

1. Clean out your closet and take your old clothes to someone in need or a shelter.

2. In church this week, tithe 10%.

3. Surprise a family member or friend with lunch on you.

# End of Day Thoughts

# Day Fifteen

"The greatest discovery of all time is
that a person can change his future
by merely changing his attitude."
Oprah Winfrey

### Devotional XV

Did you know that it is said that the average person has 6,200 thoughts per day? Yes, you read that right! Six thousand, two-hundred! Wow! What are we all thinking about?! Obviously, a ton of things. Our minds are so powerful and it is what ultimately controls how we approach our day. Starting each day with gratitude sets the tone for a day of delight, joy and peace. Starting with a negative mindset sets the tone for irritability, impatience, being grumpy and seeing things half empty. Each feeling will impact the day how you see fit. So, if we have this much control, why not set yourself up for success! If you see the glass half empty, most likely, that will be the life you live. But, if you see the glass as half full, or just FULL, you'll live a life full of optimism and gratitude. Trust me, you'll want to lead your life with the second thought! So much can and will happen for you with a mindset such as this! You'll be more patient with yourself, with others, and extend grace where need be. THIS is the life you want to live because it undoubtedly leads to a life of success and excellence! Something we should all strive for!

Do yourself a favor next time you wake up feeling like you want to shoot the day down before it even starts. Pray. Ask God to help you adjust the feelings you're feeling. Meditate on that, and then tell yourself that today will be the best day, and believe it! It won't work unless you believe it. Activate self-belief, own the shift you want to make and go make this the best day of your life.

## Activity XV

Speak these three affirmations over your life today and everyday that you feel you need to.

1. Today will be my best day yet!

2. I will be productive and make the most of my day.

3. I will keep a smile on my face and thank God for all that He's given me.

# End of Day Thoughts

# Day Sixteen

"If you find a path with no obstacles,
it probably doesn't lead anywhere."
Frank A. Clark

## Devotional XVI

Any person with goals will inevitably reach a place where obstacles reside. You can not escape it…and you shouldn't want to. This is how we grow and develop as people. Don't go around the obstacle, walk into it! Welcome it, because the obstacle will ultimately be what will strengthen your journey along the way. The lesson when facing them is learning how to overcome them!

We will all face hardships and trying times in life. If we give the obstacle that's in front of us more power than what it's worth or try to avoid them, you will without a doubt stay stagnant in life. Don't short-change yourself. Get the lesson and LEARN it. For you and your growth! The world is full of people who have faced really difficult seasons in life but come out stronger, wiser, and more aware of how to handle another obstacle that may come their way.

A life without struggles can be a life without significant change. Continue to press forward and never stop challenging yourself.

# Activity XVI

Recall a time in your life when you were challenged with something that was difficult. How did you overcome it? How do you feel now that you were able to prevail and press forward? Write about it and celebrate an important win in your life.

# End of Day Thoughts

# Day Seventeen

"Optimism is a faith that leads to success."
Bruce Lee

## Devotional XVII

Having hope and confidence in something you have yet to experience is the beauty of being optimistic! You believe in your heart that it …whatever it is you're believing in…will be…and that is such a beautiful feeling! When you think positive, it leads to incredible change in your life, and you see every opportunity God presents to you as it shall be and will be done, and without a single doubt! You expect the best, give your very best and have faith that everything will be exactly as it's supposed to be!

If you can help it at all, try your BEST to approach LIFE this way! With optimism, an abundance of faith and hope, and walk confident in knowing that God has provided you with all the tools that's needed to succeed in His calling over your life! Because, YOU. DO!

Leading your life in such a way does nothing but add value to your existence! Own your power and the story of your success!

## Activity XVII

1. Name two things you are optimistic about.

2. What steps are you taking to make sure these two things are successful?

Say this prayer: *"For I know the plans I have for you, declares the Lord, plans for welfare and not for evil, to give you a future and a hope."*
Jeremiah 29:11

# End of Day Thoughts

# Day Eighteen

"But seek first the kingdom of God,
and His righteousness, and all these
things will be added to you."
Matthew 6:33

### Devotional XVIII

Making a move before God says move is SO detrimental to His plan He has for you and your life! Trust me, I have learned the hard way over and over… and over again! I have tried doing things on my own or in my own way time and time again only to receive temporary highs and no real sense of fulfillment. When we do this, we are only making things harder for ourselves. Going through unnecessary hardships, prolonging the promises God has on our lives and take thee longest route possible to achieve them. All we simply have to do is allow God to take the wheel and we trust and follow His ordained steps that He has for us.

Doing things my way for so long, I started to feel as if I was on a hamster wheel. Going nowhere fast, seeing the same results over and over again. Nothing was new. Nothing was changing. Reading the same chapter numerous times until one day, I decided to take my hands off the wheel and allow God to steer me. I was used to being in control. Controlling the narrative of my life, how I wanted things to be, how I wanted to represent myself, etc. But when I was in control, I could only take myself so far. Releasing control was scary and I was afraid I'd grab hold again, but after being sick and tired of being sick and tired, I knew I couldn't go back to that way of living or that way of thinking. I knew I needed God more. It was time for reconstruction over my life and for me to finally allow God in the way He wanted to be all along. Turns out, it was the number one, best decision I've ever made in my whole life!

Take it from me, a stubborn, had to be in control, stuck in her own way-woman. Someone who has seen the errors in her ways, learned from them and knows the purpose of seeking God first in every decision-making process I have moving forward. God has never steered me wrong or failed me, but has made me into a woman I am proud to face in the mirror each day. When you trust God with your life, He will give you a brand new one. Do yourself a favor, seek Him in all things. You will never regret it.

## Activity XVIII

Pray and ask God to release you of all control that you have over your life for His control instead. Be specific in the areas you need it most. Meditate on this prayer with music, candle light and 10 mins of intentionality.

# End of Day Thoughts

# Day Nineteen

*"That some achieve great success, is proof to all that others can achieve it as well."*
Abraham Lincoln

### Devotional XIX

Success. What does that word mean to you and how does it position itself in your life currently? Success wears many hats, has many faces, and most certainly can not be boxed into one specific category. Success looks and feels different to everyone; but one thing is for sure, everyone can most certainly achieve it, if, they are willing to work for it.

The Oxford dictionary defines success as *"the accomplishment of an aim or purpose."* Having a vision, a dream and being passionate about it can create great success in the future. But you must know that being successful means having intentional preparation towards your dream and working at it day in and day out. It takes a ton of sacrifice, drive, discipline and determination to create success. You just have to be willing to go the extra mile and without any excuses to achieve it. People who wake up before everyone else and is the last one to go to bed at night to make their dreams come true will triumph and conquer all that they have set out to achieve and that creates success. How have you set yourself apart? Have you gone the extra mile for your goals? Are you doing all that you can to create a successful life? Answer those questions and honestly. If you are, awesome job; keep going! But, if you aren't, ask yourself why and what you are willing to modify to change this narrative.

Ultimately, it is up to you how successful you want to be in life. You can go as far as God has predestined for you! Give yourself every opportunity to do so, because success and greatness is within ALL of us! Tap into it and give it all you got!

# Activity XIX

1. Write down your biggest dream in life.

2. Create a vision board just for that dream.

3. Find someone who is already successful in this field and ask them to mentor you.

# End of Day Thoughts

# Day Twenty

"God, grant me the serenity to accept the things I cannot change, courage to change the things I can, and the wisdom to know the difference."
Reinhold Niebuhr

## Devotional XX

Oftentimes in life, we try to control the uncontrollable or things we have no control over and overlook or misuse what we can control. Let go of what you can't control. Take action where you can. It is wise to learn the difference and apply where necessary. Knowing the difference creates peace in your life.

We have all been in situations where this wisdom can surely be tested and we go against what we already know is impossible for us to grab hold of causing unnecessary stress, disappointment, and a false sense of hope setting an expectation of something unlikely to happen. Don't do this to yourself. Instead, embrace the fact that you have control over much in your life already!

When you sit and think of the demands we already have in life, why would we want to add more on us that will only bring confusion, disappointment and uncertainty? Let's thank God that He gave us the ability to handle and control what He has entrusted us with. Today, let go of all that you can't control and watch your life shift in the best way!

# Activity XX

Pray and ask God to help you release all that you try to be in control of that He hasn't given you. Be gentle with yourself and allow the negative emotions to flow.

# End of Day Thoughts

# Day Twenty-One

*"God doesn't call the qualified,*
*He qualifies the called!"*
1 Corinthians 1:21

## Devotional XXI

Have you ever thought to yourself, "I don't have what it takes to achieve all that I want to achieve? What makes me so special? There are others out there that are doing the very thing I feel called to do, yet, they are well known, have a huge following, and have what it takes to be more successful at that 'thing' more than I can be?"

If we're honest answering those questions, I would project that 99.99% of us would have answered YES to them. But why do we think this way? Why do we feel that we can't be blessed enough to fulfill the very thing God put on our hearts to do? Could it be that we lack faith, discipline, trust in our own abilities or have allowed fear to take root in our decision making? Often times, it can be one or two of those things, but most of the time, it's ALL of them! We shoot ourselves in the foot before even beginning the race. We tell ourselves NO before we even give ourselves a chance. Today, let this be the LAST day that you do this. We have EVERYTHING we need to fulfill all hopes and dreams and the desires that God has predestined for our greatness! You don't have to be well known or have a huge following to be successful at what you are called to do! All you need is to follow God's lead, have a willing heart, trust in what you KNOW you can do, and EXECUTE. Once you start that 'thing', you have no idea where God can take you. You just have to START!

God's favor on your life will always prevail! His favor will put you in rooms that you, on paper, wouldn't be qualified for, but when He says YES, that's ALL it takes! His YES over 1,000 no's triumphs ALL! Our God has the final say in our lives. He creates an environment for us to flourish and grow! No one can take what God has ordained for you to have, even when there are others who are extremely successful in the exact same field. What's for you is truly FOR YOU! You, just have to believe it! God is our qualifier. Start living your life with that truth and pursue what lights your heart on fire! Start now, God is waiting on you ☺

## Activity XXI

Meditate and intentionally pray for the gift(s) God has given you. Thank Him for the revelation that He has already placed on your life and actively work at your gift daily to master your craft.

# End of Day Thoughts

# Day Twenty-Two

"The difference between success and
mediocrity is all in the way you think."
Dean Francis

## Devotional XXII

Every day that we wake up, we have a choice. Many choices actually. *How do I want to show up in the world today? How will my attitude be today? While at work, will I go above and beyond today or just do enough to get by? Will I eat healthy or make bad food decisions, etc., etc.*! The list goes on and on. While I'm only naming a few of the choices that we make throughout our day, ultimately the current decisions we make now will be what shapes our life.

The clear difference between mediocrity and success are your daily habits. Successful people work towards their goals whereas mediocre people make excuses as to why they can't. You have to WANT success as much as you want to breathe.

It can't be driven when motivation strikes, but by disciplining yourself to make non-negotiables as to why you MUST work towards the success of your future every day. Self-discipline starts in your mind. You have to mentally tell yourself, every day, that you have the ability to pursue your goals without being easily distracted by things that will take you off course. Literally, every day, because it's a mental battle. It takes tremendous will power to become successful, but just know, you CAN make it happen.

Daily practices become your daily habits. Practice the habits of a successful person until it becomes a part of your daily routine. You can do this!

## **Activity XXII**

1.  Prioritize self-improvement. Create a to-do list.

2.  Make sure you exercise at least 30 minutes today.

3.  Work on something you're passionate about.

# End of Day Thoughts

# Day Twenty-Three

*"One detour doesn't cancel your destination."*
Sarah Jakes Roberts

### Devotional XXIII

Roadblocks are a part of life. They are what "make" the journey and what strengthen us as people. On the journey to greatness, we may encounter many of them along the way, but as many detours as we may experience in life, there is ALWAYS another way to reach our destiny!

In my life, I have experienced so many twists and turns, setbacks and roadblocks, distractions, and temptations that have kept me at square one for many years! When you are trying to lead your life the way you want and not the way God has ordained for you, you will without a doubt experience everything that I have just mentioned because doing things this way isn't the blueprint for your life. Going against what God predestined halts your journey for as long as you try to control it. God will put us in a holding place UNTIL we SEE and LISTEN to what He is trying to tell and show us. You'll try to go another way and another way until you finally see yourself on this hamster wheel that is inevitable leading you nowhere fast. Planted in the same place because you're trying to do things your own way instead of His way. While you may have taken the road that's ALWAYS traveled, and decide to finally take the detour that leads you exactly where you are supposed to be, you'll soon discover that just because you went the wrong way for a while doesn't mean that God can't get you right back on track, as if you never detoured at all, and show you that He will always have a way to bring you to His promised place for us.

Life isn't cancelled because we went left when we should have gone right. You can always make that U-turn and get back on track!

## Activity XXIII

What direction are you going towards that you know isn't the right way, but you're apprehensive to adjust because you're afraid of the unknown? Pray and ask God to strengthen your faith in this area and to help you with turning the direction of your life.

# End of Day Thoughts

# Day Twenty-Four

*"There is no reason to have a plan B because it distracts from plan A."*
Will Smith

## Devotional XXIV

Subconsciously, we all make additional plans in life "just in case" the first one doesn't work out the way we want without even recognizing that we are giving ourselves a way out of purpose and into comfortability. Plan A IS the way, we just have to plan for success, disciplining ourselves in areas that challenge us to succeed the way we know we can.

You ever sit and think, and come to the realization that you may be overly ambitious or over zealous in your pursuit to be great that you emerge yourself into things you have no business dabbling in? I laugh out loud as I write this because I know I have. I felt that I was good at so many things and wanted to do them all! I would try my hand in one thing until it was no longer exciting, and then tried my hand in something else until that fizzled away as well. I believe this stemmed from not wanting to be boxed in any way and telling myself that I can do anything I want because I was smart and caught on to things pretty fast. But, as cool as that can be at times, being good at everything means you will be a master of nothing. Once that sunk in, I really wanted to dive in on what I knew I was truly passionate about and learn different avenues in that field that gave me different outlets while mastering Plan A. Just because Plan A is one thing doesn't mean it has to be one dimensional.

A way to keep Plan A exciting is to continue to invest in it, learning different things and exploring every avenue it has to offer. Understand that it's never ending, always unfolding and will always have something new to offer.

## Activity XXIV

Name 3 things that excite you about Plan A

1.

2.

3.

List why they excite you and how you can expand each interest.

# End of Day Thoughts

# Day Twenty-Five

"Shoot for the moon. Even if you
miss, you'll land among the stars."
Norman Vincent Peale

## Devotional XXV

*"The sky is the limit!"* A phrase we have heard all of our lives, however, God doesn't limit our dreams, which means that they can go far past the sky; they can reach as high as the moon and stars, because doing anything with God will always surpass all that we can even fathom or imagine.

When on your journey to making your dreams come true, always aim as high as possible! Let your passion be the driving force in the pursuit of accomplishing goals that are bigger than yourself and will make an impact on the world! That's how BIG our dreams should be! Dreams that will shake up the world in an effort to help others be their best!

And when you shoot as high as the moon and stars, that's exactly what you'll do!

No matter where we came from, where we are starting from or how we'll get to where we are going, God will always take us to a place we never could have imagined for our lives because that's how big He is! Small thinking keeps us in small places. Think and dream BIG!

## Activity XXV

Go for a walk or run in your neighborhood. Listen to calming music and imagine all of your dreams coming true. What does that look like for you? How does that make you feel? Speak it out loud and own it. It's yours if you believe it.

# End of Day Thoughts

# Day Twenty-Six

*"Passion is energy. Feel the power that comes from focusing on what excites you."*
Oprah Winfrey

### Devotional XXVI

There is NO better feeling than FINALLY knowing what sets your SOUL on fire! It's one of the best feelings in the world to know what your driving force is in life! You'll know what this 'thing' is because it will be all that you want to emerge yourself in!

Purpose without passion simply has no substance. You lack discipline, drive, and focus. Being passionate about your purpose leads to SUCCESS! Imagine having an apathetic mindset about God's divine direction for your life. You will miss all blessings attached to your purpose and in your life because you would have surrendered to a life of mediocrity never having the grit to tap into something that's bigger than yourself, yet settling for a life that doesn't challenge you or bring out the highest vibrations possible when you don't follow His plan for your life. Never settle for safe! Yet, be ok with the unknown so that you can discover exactly you are passionate about. Try new things and be willing to go outside your normal routine. This is how you discover purpose. Once you've tapped in and you have that 'thing' that gives you so much LIFE, THIS is when it's time to take off and give it all you've got!

Your PURPOSE is your POWER and that energy is UNMATCHED! Continue to nourish the gift God has given you and never take for granted the blessing of being in His provision for your life.

# Activity XXVI

On your drive home today, take a different route and listen to easy listening music. What new did you discover? What did you see? How did going against your normal routine make you feel. Write about it.

# End of Day Thoughts

# Day Twenty-Seven

"Greatness exists in all of us."
Will Smith

## Devotional XXVII

God did not create "special" people and they only have access to greatness. He created us ALL to exude greatness! It's something that truly exists in each and every one of us!

Ultimately, what will separate you from achieving and tapping into greatness will be your work ethic. What you are willing to put into each day determines the outcome for that day. Same with life. What you are willing to give each day WILL determine the kind of life you will have. If you feel as if you are living an unfilled life, ask yourself these two questions: *What is important to me and who do I want to be?* Knowing these two, very critical things can help you on your way to greatness because knowing who you are holds SO much POWER! The direction of your life stems from TRULY knowing who you are! That's how we get from where we are to where we want to be knowing the core of our being. You stop seeing things as obstacles but as opportunities for success by bridging the gap between can't and will. It all can be so simple, yet, society has brainwashed us into thinking that this side of life heeds complexity and impossibility and because of this many of us have suppressed our greatness. Don't believe the hype! You are magnificent and wonderfully made and you have something to contribute to this world!

Continue to work on yourself, setting daily challenges, weekly goals and continue to learn by watching motivational videos, listening to inspiring podcasts and reading the word for daily mental growth. This is how change happens and how transformation takes place! Shifting your mind to reach for greater heights so that you can become the best YOU that you can be! Believe in yourself! That awakens your greatness! And know that you can achieve everything you're willing to work for!

Now, release your greatness into this world and ignite YOUR gift. Watch out world, because here you come!

## Activity XXVII

Today, be of service to someone. Try to choose someone that has a full plate and ease their day by taking a few things off to help them navigate the remainder of the day. God has blessed us to be a blessing.

# End of Day Thoughts

# Day Twenty-Eight

"For nothing will be impossible with God."
Luke 1:37

## Devotional XXVIII

God can do exceedingly and abundantly above all that we could ever imagine. We just have to BELIEVE that He can! There is no obstacle that's too big or challenging for God to turn around for our good. Things happen FOR us, not *to* us and that's to teach and strengthen our faith in Him. God wants our trust. He longs for relationship with us so that He may bring out the very best in us. We cannot do that on our own.

Perhaps, you're experiencing a difficult season in life; you're feeling stuck, overwhelmed, the weight of the world on your shoulders, as if you're backed up against a wall and have not one solution in sight. Or, maybe you feel as if you're on an emotional rollercoaster, on a hamster wheel, always ending up where you started from, and you're wanting so badly to move forward but have no idea how to. You start to question if things will ever get better, and if so, how? Well, from experience, this is when God does His best work!

God is here for you to talk to and lean on, to cover and carry you, but most importantly, to GUIDE you. Have faith in His words and TRUST Him. Things won't always make sense to you in the moment, but just know that no matter what the situation is, stand firm in knowing that's God's got you and He always will. Be patient and less anxious and allow God to show Himself strongly in your life. Embrace knowing that on this journey called life, nothing you will ever face ends in impossibility because you have God and He will forever show you that ALL things are possible…and believe that. He will always make the impossible, possible.

## Activity XXVIII

What is presently in your life, in this moment, that seems impossible to complete? It can be anything!

What is something that once seemed impossible to complete, but you've completed?

Let's bridge the gap. How did you come to a place where you wanted to tackle what seemed impossible beforehand and ended up back at a place impossibility exists again?

# End of Day Thoughts

## Day Twenty-Nine

*Be your own G.O.A.T.*
A.W. Ramsey III

### Devotional XXIX

For those of you who are unfamiliar with the acronym for the word "goat" it simply means "Greatest of all Time." It's used quite often when we hear of people who are exceptional at their craft (typically in sports), people who have paved the way to make things better for others in a historic way, or just someone who has performed in a certain field better than anyone else has. To be the G.O.A.T means to be the BEST and that's what we all should strive for!

In reality, none of us should ever start a new journey in our lives not wanting to bring our very best! We should go in wanting to give 110% of ourselves day in and day out bringing our best efforts to the table. With that said, usually when we get to choose our careers, we enter in with this mindset, but when our careers are chosen for us (meaning, it wasn't your life's dream to be at where you are, but the salary takes care of your family) we typically do well, but don't give that position everything that we can. You have to understand this. Everything that we have in life at this moment isn't forever. Somethings are simply for a season. God will put us in places where we HAVE to count on him and nothing else to take you to that place you are predestined to be. But know this, God will NOT take you there until you are ready and are grateful for where He has you right NOW, so that when it's time to go where your destined to be, all glory will go directly to HIM! While you are in your waiting season, you are to show up to that company as if you started it from the ground up! Intentionally great and giving all of yourself to service someone or something else. It's never just about us or what WE want, it's about the bigger picture at hand. Always! So, until that sinks in, prepare for a longer waiting season.

Now, this isn't to punish you, but to have you depend more on God, and not just focus on what you want. God will give us all that our heart desires, but being a G.O.A.T. means to think outside of YOU, because that come with temporary praise.

Being your own G.O.A.T. means to be bring your best at ALL that's assigned to your life, not just what you choose. Keep this in mind when you feel the struggles of your current season. Being the best doesn't come with ease, but the sacrifices that it takes to get there are always worth the wait.

# Activity XXIX

## How to be the G.O.A.T.

1.  Eliminate distractions.

2.  Allow mistakes to be teachable lessons.

3.  Discipline yourself.

4.  Dream BIG

# End of Day Thoughts

# *Day Thirty*

"I'm releasing older, lesser versions
of myself while allowing the
greatness inside of me to shine."
Danielle Nicole Ramsey

### Devotional XXX

Gone are the days where we diminish our light so that we can stay stagnant in a place of comfort that no longer serves us! Yes indeed! From this day forward, we are moving in a direction where we release strongholds of fear, insecurity, uncertainty, and self-sabotage, having the audacity to stand tall walking in faith knowing God is with us through it all!

Standing in your own way is a REAL THING; and a lot of us are very good at it! We can be so fearful of the unknown being greater than what we are used to that we sabotage ourselves, unintentionally, reverting back to what we are familiar and ...dare

I say it...comfortable with. Being in your comfort zone is a dangerous place to be in. It cripples you and prevents any chance of you fulfilling your life's purpose. We are MORE than capable of improving our lives and achieving all that we dream of. God has equipped us with everything we need to see things through.

When moving forward, be sure to not focus so much on the outcome; that can become very detrimental and cause us to want to give up, but instead focus on the journey, making small steps towards something great! Enjoy the present moment of taking steps towards a life where you are releasing yourself from things of the past, making excuses with justification, and limiting your belief in your capabilities. Look in the mirror and know that divine greatness is within you and you hold the power to set it free!

The old me is gone and the new me is a version of myself that allows for great things to flow into my life! I don't purposely hold myself back, I'm letting go of self-doubt, I take action of all that I control in my life and I know that just by simply being alive that greatness has a place for me! Today, I'm choosing to make my mark in this world by trusting that what God has for me, is truly for me, and to start living the life I've always imagined!

## Activity XXX

Take a look at who you are close to in your life. Your key people. Your squad. Are they all for you, or pretend to be? When you are around these people, do you feel inspired, or do you diminish yourself to fit in? I ask, because igniting the greatness inside of you means you need to have a winning team with you! These are your go-to people! They HAVE to reflect direction your life is going. Take a moment to write their names down, and give each of them a thumbs up…or down and why.

# End of Day Thoughts

# *Outro*

Congratulations!

You've officially completed Volume I of this amazing trilogy! I hope you are proud of yourself and that you feel renewed walking into the next season of your life! You have prepared for purpose and the mindset shift has been made! You are not the same person you were when you began this devotional!

Now, you are stepping in to your purpose and my hope is that you continue to encourage yourself with self-development, create intentional time with God, and continue to improve your way of thinking.

# FitnessDani

CHANGING LIVES INSIDE & OUT

Made in the USA
Monee, IL
10 April 2022

94460794R00075